Adventures with Mimi

Evalee Searches for Clancy

Written by
Jordan Petter

Illustrated by
Lidia Fernández Abril

Note from the Author

Individuals come from all walks of life; our different experiences and the places we live influence how we speak and the unique ways we use language. Throughout my book, you may encounter a word that seems unfamiliar to you.

'Tank' – Several southerners use the word 'tank.' In our region, size-wise, a pond refers to an extremely small body of water. Next in size is a tank; this is a body of water one would likely see on a person's property or ranch with livestock drinking from it. The next size up is a lake, and after that would come bays and oceans.

Copyright ©2025 Jordan Petter
Written by Jordan Petter
Illustrated by Lidia Fernández Abril

Photo of Jordan Petter by Denise Petter
Photo on Dedication Page by Maroney Photography
Photo of Lidia Fernández Abril (self-photo)

Published by Miriam Laundry Publishing Company
miriamlaundry.com

HC ISBN 978-1-77944-274-1
PB ISBN 978-1-77944-273-4
e-Book ISBN 978-1-77944-272-7

FIRST EDITION

To our beautiful daughters,
Evalee and Dalynn—

May God guide your path and bless
you with love, joy, and wisdom as you
journey through life.

When Momma and Daddy leave to haul some cows to the sell barn, Evalee stays at the ranch with her grandma. Hanging out with Mimi is always fun, especially when they get to explore!

"Can we go to the pasture and check the other cows now, Mimi?" Evalee asks.

"Ab-so-tute-a-loot-ly!" Mimi replies. "Let's grab some cubes and a bale of hay they can munch on."

Evalee hurries to the hay barn and unlocks the gate. Mimi backs up the buggy and helps Evalee load the feed.

With the wind in their hair and the sun kissing their skin, Evalee and Mimi begin searching for the herd.

"Honk your horn, Mimi!" Evalee exclaims. "That'll get 'em coming!"

HONK! HONK!

They ride around the pasture, through the
brush, and under the outstretched trees.

MOO!

"Mimi! I see them!" Evalee points and her smile widens. "It's the best sound in the world, isn't it?"

Mimi grins, looking over at Evalee's face — bright from the sun, but even brighter with joy.

As they get closer, Mimi's smile fades. "Hmm," she murmurs. "Five of our cows are missing, including Clancy."

Clancy is Evalee's favorite cow. She is always gentle, letting Evalee feed and even pet her!

"Let's spread out the hay and cubes for these cows," Mimi says. "Then we'll go find the others."

Mimi grabs the bag of cubes while Evalee throws out flakes of hay. Hearing the bag rustle makes the cattle trot a little faster toward Mimi.

"Mimi? Can we save some for the other cows?" Evalee frowns. "They've gotta be hungry, too."

"Good idea, Sweetie," Mimi replies as she rolls up what's left of the cube bag and stuffs it in the buggy. "Load up!"

As they bounce along, Evalee asks, "Where do you think the other cows are?"

"I'm not sure. Keep your eyes peeled."

Evalee twists her head and scrunches her nose at Mimi. Mimi has always had an odd way of explaining things, but Evalee gives an understanding nod, and squints, as if focusing on the horizon.

"Look! I think I see them!" Evalee points to a large oak tree on the fence line. "Oh, no! The fence is down and our cows are on the other side! And where's Clancy?!"

Mimi parks the buggy, and they both get out to inspect the fence. "With the cows in the neighbor's pasture, it's going to be difficult getting them back on our land," Mimi explains.

Evalee is worried that something is wrong with Clancy. *Cows travel in herds, Evalee tells herself. Clancy should've been here, too.*

"Evalee!" Mimi snaps Evalee's attention back to the current situation. "Come around the back side of them and let's get 'em back in the pasture."

Evalee does as she is told, but trips over a broken tree limb. The commotion frightens the cattle, and they scurry in the opposite direction.

"MOOOOO."

Evalee and Mimi try calling them, but they keep running away!

17

Evalee remembers the bag of cubes. She hurries to the buggy, and shakes the bag with all her might. Soon, the cows are trotting toward her! Evalee crosses onto their property, with the cows following right behind her.

"Look at you, Evalee!" Mimi yells. "That's my girl!"

Once the cows are back on their side, Evalee and Mimi mend the broken fence. "As good as new," Mimi says, as they admire their work.

"We've still gotta find Clancy, Mimi! I'm worried about her."

They sprinkle a few cubes and toss a flake of hay out for the cows, then hop in the buggy.

Through the trees, around the tanks, and over the hills they scour for Evalee's most adored cow.

"Mimi! Stop!" Evalee shouts, pointing in the direction of an old, rusted shed that the cattle use for protection against the weather. "There she is!"

Clancy is lying under the shed, resting her head on the ground.

Evalee sees something dark lying on the ground next to Clancy.

A small ball of fur begins to squirm, and a tiny head appears.

"It's a baby, Mimi!"
Evalee exclaims.

"Would you look at that!"
Mimi says, relieved.

"Can I pet it?"
Evalee asks eagerly.

"We'd better not, Sweetie. It's
best to just leave them alone."

"But I love Clancy, and
now I love her baby!"

"I know you do," Mimi reassures her, "but Clancy needs to care for her new calf. The calf doesn't know you, and we don't want to frighten it."

Evalee sighs. "I guess so." Her lip begins to quiver.

Mimi leans in, "Even though we can't pet it, would you still like to give it a name?"

Evalee's eyes brighten. "Ab-so-tute-a-loot-ly!"

They inch closer to Clancy and her new calf. Half of its face is blocked by Clancy's, but Evalee is able to see its glossy eyes slowly open and stare up at them.

"What would you like to call it?" Mimi asks.

Evalee inspects the new calf. *Brownie? Lucky? Starry?* she thinks, but doesn't like the way they sound. Then, Clancy moves her head and...

27

There! On the calf's upper lip is some white hair in the shape of a mustache. "That's it!" Evalee tells Mimi. "Her name is Stache."

"Perfect!" Mimi declares.

Evalee remembers the bag of cubes and flakes of hay they saved. "Clancy's gotta be hungry after having the baby, right?" Evalee asks Mimi. "Can we give her the rest of the cubes and hay?"

"That's a great idea," Mimi responds.

Evalee's face beams as she disperses the feed on the ground for Clancy.

Evalee and Mimi drive back to the house, talking about the unexpected events of the morning.

Evalee smiles. "I wonder if Momma and Daddy are back from the sell barn," she says. "I can't wait for them to meet Stache!"

Evalee leans in close to Mimi, feeling the warmth of her love, and wonders if Stache feels the same bond with Clancy. *Ab-so-tute-a-loot-ly,* she decides.

About the Author

Jordan Petter is an award-winning and bestselling author who was born, raised, and currently resides in Texas. Her love for reading and writing began as a child and progressively grew during her early adulthood. When she's not writing or working as a campus librarian, she spends most of her time with her family, including her husband and their two daughters. Jordan enjoys traveling, the outdoors, and attending athletic events.

Jordan aspires to enlighten young readers to a world full of curiosity and joy by writing adventurous children's books. Her debut children's book, *Evalee Goes Fishing*, is the first in the *Adventures with Mimi* series.

Connect with her at **www.jordanpetterauthor.com**

About the Illustrator

Lidia Fernández Abril is a freelance illustrator from Spain. Since she was a child, her passion has been drawing and painting, creating stories, and developing characters.

She started her professional career in the animation film industry, working for Spanish movies such as *The Cid* and *Planet 51*, but nowadays she is focused on illustrating children's books, a field that she loves.

She really enjoys the process of telling stories with her drawings, whether it is for a children's book, a graphic novel, a movie, or a game. This is why she tries to learn as much as possible on every project she approaches.

Portfolio Online: **www.advocate-art.com/lidia-fernandez**
Instagram: **@lidix_art**

www.ingramcontent.com/pod-product-compliance
Lightning Source LLC
LaVergne TN
LVHW072115070426
835510LV00002B/69